AN ATTIC
OF IDEALS

AN ATTIC
OF IDEALS
Karen Swenson

DOUBLEDAY & COMPANY, INC.
GARDEN CITY, NEW YORK   1974

Some of these poems first appeared in publications: *The Quarrel* and
The Girl Friend, *Antioch Review*, Copyright © 1968, 1969 by Antioch
Review, Incorporated, respectively; *Why Didn't Anyone Tell Hester
Prynne? Beloit Poetry Journal*, Copyright © 1971 by Beloit Poetry
Journal; *The Moon* and *A Family*, *Denver Quarterly*, Copyright © 1970
by The University of Denver; *Moon Walk, Epos; The Visit* and *Bridges,
The Nation; Woman: Gallup, N.M.* and *Farewell to Fargo: Selling the
House, The New Yorker; A T Joint, New York Poetry*, Copyright ©
1970 by Entelechy Press; *Dear Elizabeth, Prairie Schooner*; three poems,
*The Barmaid and the Alexandrite, Impressions, The Death of A Photog-
rapher, Quarterly Review of Literature*, Copyright © 1970 by Quarterly
Review of Literature; *The Portrait, Shenandoah; The Quilt, The Smith
Anthology*, Copyright © 1971 by The Smith; four poems, *Hecuba,
Hooks and Eyes, The Price of Women, The Eclipse, New American
Poetry*, edited by Richard Monaco, published 1973 by McGraw-Hill,
Inc.; *The Phosphorescent Man, Saturday Review*, Copyright © 1972 by
Saturday Review, Inc.; *Memorial Day, Texas Quarterly*, Copyright ©
1973 by University of Texas at Austin.

ISBN: 0-385-08073-5 Trade
       0-385-08081-6 Paperback
Library of Congress Catalog Card Number 73–81449
Copyright © 1967, 1968, 1969, 1971, 1973, 1974 by Karen Swenson

CONTENTS

PART TWO

PART THREE

PART ONE

The Heroines

The heroines lived with their husbands'
shelved principles
in an attic of ideals,
kept dusted the broken bowls of justice, honor,
all men hold the best
and kept in the quiet reservoir of womanhood,
a still lake where
they leaned from the shore and saw
not their faces but their faith,
because what you cannot be
must still belong to you.

The heroines kept the attics clean
because they believed
the attic was nirvana,
that man could alchemize them into inexistence,
but they were only caretakers,
dusters of undone deeds,
only ladies adrift in the lake.
Ophelia, innocence offended, sang bawdy songs
and drowned in the attic.

The Empress of Forever

We could, of course, stuff her in her sequins
and put her behind glass with a neat label —
          DIETRICH
          Semper Sexualis —
this carnal fairy tale on stage in the Tivoli.

Her face has been operated into existence.
Her figure, plastic as an airline dinner,
lurks nudely within her gown's frozen torch,
a sun icicle, licking the length of her legs.
Her voice husks through forty years of song,

as in the stage dust
sentiment and roses mellow
as the empress of forever takes her bow.

Virginia

First they took off one breast
then the other
then her ovaries came out
then her pituitary gland.

Slowly they dismembered her
to keep her alive.
They started with the things they understood
cutting her womanhood away,
the most obviously infected part,
and then the module
whose function they weren't sure of.
It is a matter of taking out the fuse
so the lights won't go on.

She stands on the corner and talks to me,
wearing her scars behind the soft sculpture of foam,
tells me that living with death is not too bad.
It gives life salt, not depending
on any other time to make up your tense,
and days become what they always should have
been pungent with the present.

She leaves me to go to the hospital,
moving from biopsy to biopsy
as they cut her back to the bone,
but the more they minus
the more multiples there are.

Dear Elizabeth:

We are almost all homely,
beauty being rare as a round stone,
and I was once homelier than thou,
> pocked teeth, long nose, plain geometry jaw,
> an unleavened matzo angling down the street,
> pigeon-toed strip of bespectacled lath.

The swan's story is a sweet one,
but it is a puff-ball beast.
Robin's April pretty, live on worms
to become unnoticeable by June.
> But the hatched hawk, gall-eyed
> in clumsy fluff between feet and beak,
> lives on fought flesh — waiting
> for shoulders to lean upon the wind.

I tell you this to keep comfort till your time.
A man is held stronger by beauty he knows
than any loveliness his eye can see.
> And don't mind Helen with Grecian ships,
> that is the male's most fervent legend,
> told by a wanderer totally blind.

The Barmaid and the Alexandrite

Route 66, a rut of scenery and cigarettes —
all I know of Indianapolis
is a lady's room at 3 A.M.

I slept with strangers.
The mornings, born green,
were honed down by the sun

to my cigarette —
one spark on the night window

as the telephone pole tally
ticked down to Flagstaff,
a bed, a bath, a bar and there

her round arms, pale,
moonlit adobe dreams,
passed the beers down the bar.

With a smile like a torn billboard
she moved through male voices
from Tucumcari, to Gallup, to Flagstaff.

Desert towns isolated on the land, bright and brittle,
as a potato chip bag caught on a cactus.

The night slackened to a shade of New York City snow
and the last pair of cowboy boots measured
their metronome stride on the dew-darkened sidewalk.

Stirring her coffee she talked —
boardinghouses, suitcases,
wild daisies wilting in a peanut-butter jar.

And then she reached into her bra,
undid a safety pin, and set in my hand
the ring, a welt of color warm from her skin —

an alexandrite, heliotrope-heavy in the half-light.
Two women in the dirty laundry dawn
hunched over a stone.

Silence circled from the cold desert
to slither the edge of our skirts.

We watched the stone waver in the mizzling sun
as its color curdled to green in my hand —
jelled green in the first sparrow call.

I left on the bus to find my way back
home — the honeycomb that fits you into all its holes —
gnawed my way back through hamburgers

and the anonymous arteries of America
trying to read answers in road signs.

And she passed out the beers
wearing a stone against her breast;
a dark bruise that she watched

resolve again to green in every dawn
from Telluride, to Taos, to Galisteo.

The Girl Friend

Father ate rat poison one night in bed
and curled around the can, like a kid with his teddy bear,
until the morning when they straightened him out.

Mother calls up the FBI
to report communists in the candystore
and sees obscene couples incessantly
in uncurtained windows.

They stain her mind like chicken fat
as she watches chewing her gumdrops.

While in another part of town
the daughter calls us every night.
(I am only one on a long comfort list.)

She attics our ears with the gimcrack details of her day —
the dime lost in the laundromat —
the receptionist who forgets messages —
the man who smiled on the other side of the bridge table.

Breath bitter with the placenta of her parents' lives,
her mouth shuffles like feet stifled in newspapers.

We hand her gently between our voices
as though she were a restless child until
she dwindles into the void of her sleeping pill.

Then we smile at our husbands,
and go to the kitchen to finish the dishes.
The bottoms of our pots exclaim our faces
brilliant and misshapen as the chewed nickel of pity.

Waiting for Monday

She lives with her baby,
alone for the summer in Bridgehampton,
in a house between an old woman who coughs,
and another who drinks,
only a walk from the beach.

When the birds sing morning about the house
she gets up and feeds her son,
plays with his make-believe fingers
and talks to his silence and the rented walls
until her husband comes for the weekend.

They make love and her leased walls
stiffen into collars of windowless starch
she cannot jump from.
Though she cannot plagiarize his hands
into the fantasies of other lovers
she would have his hands be others.

Carefully she kneads her restlessness to passion
and waits,
for her son's voiceless palms —
the silent demand of toys her mother gave her —
for Monday,
when the walls will enlarge again into loneliness
only a walk from the beach.

The Quilt

Alive in a brown stucco house
picketed by thorns of a barberry hedge
(in fall their berries spattered red
as a smashed Christmas ball)

she sat at the front window in
a horsehair rocker sleek as
the bottoms of her pots and pans.

She hated as she dug the needle
into the widening pattern of the quilt —
a patchwork of her deciduous dresses

radiating from the center of satin,
white stone cast first.
The memories of material
spread their circles around it.

A swatch of evening dress never worn.
A rectangle of the coat she made herself.
She pinned them and pierced them,

fettering the failures together
with a tense silk thread,
cross stitch, blanket stitch, chain stitch,

her embroidery precise as the steel shaft.
When the design was updated by
the lining of her worn-out suit,
she smoothed the quilt across their bed.

A Family

Voice muggy with affection and coffee cake
she keeps her sons arranged;
one against the bookcase,
the other at the piano,
with her smile darned like her nightgown

while her husband on the wall
scuttles behind the pulp of his paintings.
Still cobwebbed by the lines of his last revolt

the sinews of his parents' care
support his Brooklyn Bridge —
little white tentacles, like mold
against a tomato sunset.

She licks her finger under the lamplight,
blots the crumbs up from the table.
She has always been satisfied.

That satisfaction wraps around them,
a bandage of all the lace her nightgown never had,
knotted to the torn sheets that cleaned the windows.

And when she rises
sucking the last crumb from her finger
to meet the challenge of their hunger again,
the nightgown swings, swings,
a pendulum on the back of the bathroom door.

Hooks and Eyes

Irish lace and linen —
she had the design right,
the skirt's mountain laurel pucker,
but no hooks and eyes.

So she sewed me in,
a last-minute needle
through my first communion —
my marriage to Christ.

The next time it was grandma's
pale wedding gown,
a supple splurge of curdled satin.

Her damned needle basted me in again,
a lean noose loop.
Through a succession of dresses
her loose stitch has pulled

pattern and fabric to the scissor's mouth.
Only now I realize
that's what she's always done;
gathered me into the paradigm, a slack abstract.

I bend my coffin cloth of flesh
basted hem to skin.
She's forgotten the hooks and eyes
again, and sewed me in.

The Moon

Their footprints on her face —
you could tell they enjoyed marking her up.

I have seen my son the same,
a joy of sloshing galoshes
across a brisk sheen of new snow.

It's something in the male;
they can't stand just openness.

They have to put things into it —
a flag, a rocket, a foot,
any signature of their spore.

Being female, I felt sorry for her.
Not that it will make any difference

to lovers and harvests and I do realize
we may need her some day, a steppingstone
for some new hypocrisy of hope

as we put distance between ourselves
and our latest botch of civilization.

But did the deflowering have to
be so public? Did we have to wave
the bloodied sheet? Columbus was kinder.

This is a very female point of view,
I realize, foolish, even sentimental.

But it hurt, woman to woman,
to see their footprints on her face,
for women are, after all, only space.

Woman: Gallup, N.M.

The shadow of her profile lay stringent
across the step of curb,
a styptic etch against his blood,

and he silent beside her,
lesions pale in the scars
of his limp hands.

The baby against
the breathing of her breast
watched, with black eyes
from under a ruffled lambchop hat,

the bus passengers walk
arranged oblivion in and out.

They did not talk.
She yielded him nothing but rigid back;
her neck a carved anger of tendons
where the black down murmured.

God! what had he done
that could not be darned with tears?

She sat lizard dry.
Road and railroad ran through her head.
The land ate red
to a frail mirage of mountains.

He raised his head
and with a gentleness of hand,
hesitant as settling dust,
stroked the curve of her neck.

His motion was only man to woman.
It was not enough.
Her silhouette, knifed out of sunlight,
fell into the gutter.

The passengers walked over it,
and she was mute as snakeskin.

If he had cast himself into his own
shadow under the bus wheel
she would not have wept
or cracked her parched profile,

until night erased it
or the baby gummed a pale cry.
He reached out again,
a cramped consent of fingers
down her shoulder.

His arm, opening
to press the baby's head against
the hollow of her collarbone,
scythed back into his breath.

Across a red scorch to mountains
she shattered on the pavement.

The Price of Women

Every woman, you say, has her price:
a house with trees and tricycles,
a yellow porcelain sink that matches
shine to shine the kitchen cabinets,

and some are more expensive
requiring Tiffany's and other labels
draped over their luncheon chairs.

These are the bargains of love
or quiet or just another body to be by.

But are they? Isn't this the way we
counter what we will not give, a game
of poker-chip exchange — an emerald for
emotion, not an equal sign

but the ellipse of instead of —
because what would I do if
you or anyone walked into the room

in the middle of the commercial
and asked for my life?

At Ever After Inc.

They've got a suite to fit your sorrow
and a man to say the words.
You prime him the night before
and he produces your dead, a plastic favor
at the bottom of the crackerjack box of the psalms.

We stand in one room, talking, smoking,
while she lies in the next —
a taxidermist's delight.

Her hands are a thatch of cinnamon sticks
but there is no cosmetic for her nose —
it strikes against the puckered white satin.
That much dignity is left

though Jenny Strauss is dead
who wore an amethyst on her hand,
spent her honeymoon in Florence at forty,
went senile at seventy-eight and threw her shoe
through the nursing home window.

The ceremony rolls on inevitably as a banquet menu
but always just a little off —
the wrong lid on the wrong jar.

The rabbi talks of God
but we've forgotten who he is.

They close the coffin.
It clicks like a cheap suitcase.

Her face is packed, her body folded
into our ready-made mourning, but it does not fit
six feet of imitation silver handles.
She is a product of death on the assembly line
and all sorrow is out of sync.

Hecuba

Hecuba, I want to know,
behind that mask
taut and intransigent as the glaze on my best china,
what grimace did you make
when Hector at Achilles' heel flopped like a fish
over the old dishcloth heaps of other dead men.

The flies
rose and settled
rose and settled
play parachutes disturbed by chariot wheels.

Did you think how luxuriant
the grass would be next year
rooting around Troy's wall?
Or of wars and whores and how
old men pimp the prostitute of death
to watch the young men lay her?

Some women wear their dead
as generals their medals,
a decoration of their own bravery.
They were able to bear this death.

Did you put a black handkerchief around his picture
and send the maid out
for the wax smugness of a lily?

More than two thousand years later,
two thousand years of the aphorism of graves and grass
(neither eggbeaters nor philosophy change anything)

I have a son,
a minnow in time's mouth. Hecuba,
behind old Homer's blind mask,
I want to know.

Farewell to Fargo: Selling the House

Olivia is dying. Bring your best black dress.
There will be nothing to take back.
The red squirrels gnawed into all the trunks
and devoured everything in the attic.

The summons was rescinded. She still lives.
I have been called to a different funeral.

An ebony elephant. A china invalid's cup,
blue and white, fragile as the tremor of veins
warping an old hand. The dining room table
that curves into clawed brass feet.

Little heaps of leftovers under plastic,
they stand isolated,
punctuation marks without our sentence.

The purchasers walk between them,
choosing what they will reincarnate.
I can not bear the helplessness
of the objects dying from our lives.

Aimless as a mourner dismissed from the grave,
I wander out to the garage.

I climb the stairs to the loft.
There is a raw sound of scampering
in the dust before my footfalls.

I find Ferd's silver capped cane
behind the lawn mower.
He died when I was in the second grade,
a fat man in a gilt frame.

Six daughters and two sons divisible
into workers, the greedy and dreamers.

Ferd and Peter kept the store.
Olivia kept the books.
Elizabeth kept the house.

Ann painted roses on china
and grapes on canvas.
Claire, in a purple velvet gown,
played a gold harp.

Julia and Amelia moved after
the quarrel across town and
were only asked to funerals.

They've all gone to the wall, photographs,
leg-of-mutton sleeves
leaning on the porch rail.
Watch chains linked like beaded portieres.

There were rides on Sunday after mass,
parasols behind horses.
Sun honed light above the wheat.

The prairie dust silted into every ruffle.
Then they trotted back to town,
to the house harrowed between the trees,
to dinner on the mahogany table,

eating out of the shine of their faces
while the Red River, a block away,
gnawed its banks roiling northward.

And what did they ride out to see? There is no
tree, no shrub, no rise of land on the plain.

One by one, they died upstairs
under the great arm of the elm
and were taken down in narrow chests,
bumping the turn of the banister.

Now only one remains, her mind
sieved by the years to pablum, waiting
to be a name laid into the grass.
She does not know the house is sold.

I take the cane back to the house and
lay it on the dining-room table to be bought.

The purchasers are gone.
There is a storm coming.
I stand on the front step.

The elms hover over the emptied house.
Seeds snow down against the dark sky.
platelets spiraling in a quickening breeze.

Red squirrels on the roof quarrel
in the fevering silence. Chain lightning
shocks heaven into a jigsaw.

The screen door behind me screams
its spring and slams.

Nursing Home

THE CANARY

In this hospital odor
his wings behind the lacquered
brass tendons of his cage
are a pathetic fallacy,

raking away the cosmetics
of grouped vinyl chairs —
the plants arranged like
a high wax finish.

He sings into his striped
shadows of the sun,
as a wheel chair whispers
spokes down the hall.

THE DOLL

Rouge the cracked china of her cheeks.
Tie a pink ribbon in her hair.
Dress up the ninety-year-old
for a visit from her relatives.

And we come in and sit beside her,
uncomfortable at the living funeral.
She says, "Oh yes. Yes," to everything;
but her eyes fold us back gently,
pale as tissue paper.

Hidden behind the bedroom door, she
snips gold fringe from her mother's earrings,
to make a necklace for her doll's
Limoges white neck.

She strokes the ribbon in her hair
and smiles tenderly at the wall.
We leave. Flat white shoes
put her away unbroken.

THE VISIT

The wild animal fear is upon him.
Still young enough to smell
death and the cripple,
he does not want to come in
here where she lies in her crib.
But he does — guarded by the lives

of grandmother and mother,
eyes strafing the room for comfort.
Her witch-aged face turns.
The tendon raw hands reach through the bars.
Time is a membrane between their touch.
"My baby, my baby boy," she says,

pulling him into her parenthesis of steel.
"You must not call him a baby," we reprimand.
His voice is torn linen; "She can call me anything."

Could he be the face?
She laughs at us and kisses
his hair through the cage.

The Portrait

He wouldn't buy her shoes
because her family was rich.

So she washed the curds
out of the milk bottles —
love clung a sour white scab on glass —

and took the bottles back to the dairy
saving the pennies for cheap shoes.

It was only after she was crippled,
that she came home on carbuncled feet,
to live again with her brothers and sisters

in the house where the prairie wind
sloughed the last scent off the roses.

She painted their roses on their plates;
for their dining-room wall, in another frame,
blue ripples of grapes falling into their own shadows

on a tablecloth —
bloom on china — ripeness on canvas.

And again and again she painted herself,
not in a palette of poses, but always
quarter profile against a ringent background;

only shoulders and a fracture of a face,
just enough to be someone you almost knew.

When he died in a telegram
she painted herself quarter view again —
a portrait of a woman as less than one.

PART TWO

Moon Walk

My son lies a monochrome of the moon;
the moon that throws the window on the floor
marking a pale path of steppingstones.

I walk through her window to his bedside.
She has crawled into even
the small curl of his hands, coating him,
as mercury does gold, with her light.

And though we spin under her light;
a small blue gall smudged with continents,
wearing a ragged shawl of cloud,

the moon is printed with our fate —
apron stringed to us now by more
than the fishhook drag of tides.

She slips over the small corner of my clay.
Her cool alloy clings to his cheek
as I walk through her window
leaving no mark on this side of space.

The Divorced Man

Six nights of television, colored
by occasional women.

He lies askew on the bed
like the morning's coffeepot on the sink
and presses buttons that change nothing
by remote control.

On another day, in the falling leaves of Sunday love,
he takes his child to the museum;
to the Monet swings in the park, watching
his wife's face in the soliloquy of his son's smile.

The Kasha Kid

A kasha kid, fat boy of an affluent world —
mouth pursed like a plush movie seat,
wet and wondering where Mama's spoon went —
he watches the teacher's legs as a new
sweet-tooth need flickers his gut.

When he drawls his salami legs down the hall
no woman's head turns to tuck his ass into her gaze.
He drags it home alone to a kitchen chair,
to the stale cabbage perfume of mother's love.

And when the lights are out and her nightgown
binds across her breasts and dreams,
the clumsy culmination of her oatmeal and mustard plasters
sits at his darkened window with binoculars
magnifying his wetness into the gleam of other rooms.

The Death of a Photographer

Light was his paradigm:
he wove it, a cat's cradle
to knot them in, eyes rounded
to the dead instant on paper —
an 8×10 moment — glossy.

It was a trade of stealth,
the black box a trap
for the unstilted gesture;
and maybe that is why
he stole things —

ashtrays, wives, and bibles —
always in need of basics.
He had compassion for the unpossessed
objects scarred by the anonymity
of hotel rooms, never taking the new,
only those roughed with use like
the corroded edge of his pant cuff.

And the wives:
perhaps it was the stealth and
the way he saw them in secret under
the catafalque of the camera's cloth,
smiles buried upside down on

ground glass, a mask reversed;
and still their skirts were neat —

defying gravity. Like a Japanese
who has saved a life, having seen
them exposed, he felt responsible.

Late at night, after
they had left, he enlarged their faces
and watched them bloom blank paper,
a monochrome resolve, swimming from
alkali to acid. He hung them on a
clothesline and left the room
ambushed by drying smiles.

There were six wet handkerchiefs
and one dry that would not
cry here, in the cold silence
of folding chairs.
The blurred faces turned

to the clattering edge of
sunlight and walked into their
own focus, while his portrait,
in a blue blazer, was nailed
down to its dark frame.

Memorial Day

Paunches and poppies in the sun,
they march in some remembered step,
civilian feet hurting
under the sallow shade of May leaves.

Between the red plumes of the trombones
and the thighs of the drum majorettes
what are they remembering, these middle-aged men?

marching in the memory of death —
the death they did not die behind them —
the death they must die before them.

The tuba pumps like a heart pacer,
the majorette flashes her legs —
a card trick of youth —

and they are the middle men
between high school drums and death.
Banners mark time in the sun.

Grand Army Plaza

Ten o'clock at night in Brooklyn.
Ten o'clock at the Plaza of the Grand Army.

The hills of the Plaza lie salted in snow,
the barren trees reach from lamp to lamp
around the circle of apartment houses
swatched with lights,

and at the far end, the arch under searchlights
shines its mouth of neither entrance nor exit
against the nighted trees at the beginning of Prospect Park.

The arch of the Grand Army,
an imitation of the Washington Square Arch,
an imitation of the Arc de Triomphe,
imitation of the Arch of Trajan,
which imitates an infinite number of victorious openings;

and if you set them up in your imagination,
a series of croquet hoops reaching back to Adam and Eve,
who stand joined by epaulets of snow
in the fountain at the middle of the Plaza,
they are an arcade of ages
with Victory in her chariot
grassed greener than graves by the rain
always rearing her bitted horses at the top.

In the bereavement of belief more real than their lives,
they died for Grant's bronze uptown tomb,
for Lincoln's marble throne —
in armor and anger, for flags and faces they died —
for the Invalides concrete courtyard of glory,
for the Colosseum's ancient malocclused bite
against a bright sky.

Snow seasons the bulldozed man-made hills
at the Plaza of the Grand Army
and beyond no searchlight condones the trees in Prospect
     Park,
where the sky salts a wither of grass.

The Veteran

After two years of war,
after sniper silence,
after the villages bombed and built, bombed and built,
you have returned to smell of your mother's laundry soap.

Her starch glazes children, naked with foreign eyes,
pouring dust from fist to palm, from fist to palm.
She irons them into the sweet odor of your shirt
warm with steam like the potatoes
peeled marbles on the plate.

And she has
made you an Ajax image,
scrubbed and perfect as a pomegranate's skin
that denies its bleeding seeds.

One of the *ancien régime* of mothers, her only weapon
the clorox cliché that bleaches all stains
into a passive monochrome denial
that rots the fabric with its clean smell,
until she must mend the pallor of her corrosive repudiation.

But still is the dust, the children,
and other sons in silence and rifles.
Though she deny death with her darning needle
the truth remains despite love.

The Unicorn

Civilization begins with Armageddon.
The ontological absolutes
Lust
War
Chastity
trumpet mortals to arms and the ambiguity of heroism.
Before the tapestry woven by these enfranchised fates —
broken teeth of epic towers
Ilium
Heorot
Carthage —
honor breaches our bones
without the flesh of love.

When only the angleworm weaves the spring roots of grass
Ulysses sails home through tournaments of lust:
Aeneas sails from desire to death
and a queen pours wine
filling goblets as if they were grails
while the poet threads his song through his harp.

But when all armor has failed
and culture cries out for the last compassion
the last compromise of love
there is another tapestry.

In a gentle center a myth
lies serene in a circle of violets,
his ribs tender repetitions of new moons
his horn delicate as the ivory braid of a widow.
He lies pale and serene in our imagination of immortality.
Silent and gentle he lies in our fabric
in our ambiguity unowned
mortal as violets he waits and
time is the present of time, no more.

The Viking Grave at Ladby

An old whale hump of earth
it rises between plowed furrows of a farm,
a memory of violence in these peaceful fields
where only the poppies bleed wild amongst the wheat
rooted in a memory now fallow in the soil.

You enter the earth,
walk down stairs into the tomb
domed in the sun with grass and wild flowers.

And there in a glass showcase,
as though it were ordinary as an earring,
a fossil under fluorescent light,
is the boat and the bones nine hundred years old.

The planks are decomposed until they are only
a child's fingernail tracing in the dirt.

The ribs are broken,
but still the bow of triumph breaches,
a wave forever at the cupped crest,
alone out of the earth
though rot is its wake.

Between its ribs a compost heap
of bones and ornaments —
dogs, horses and gold —

sacrificed by those who knew
life must be made a gift to death
if there is to be memory.

All the bones are there but his,
the man who was worthy of sacrifice,

the man whom they wanted to live
through these animal deaths,
whom they wanted to ride
triumphant into Odin's kingdom —
heels to horse and hounds to hand.

But when Christ came on an East wind
the folk were afraid
caught between the crucifix and the sword —
between wood and steel.

They thought this man came back
a rider over the sea of eternity
on that storm a pale rider
his hounds baying at his hand

to stalk their fields
where his tomb rose among their furrows
a memory of the old belief,
a humped animal asleep under the moon.

Since they had decided to let a man die for them,
rather than die for a man,
afraid of what they had forsaken
they pled in the dark to a dead God

and to exorcise the ghost of glory
they dug the man out of the mound.

While the priest muttered the words against their fear
the church bell rang across the level fields
swallowing its own echo.
Faith desecrated faith to consecrate.

Shivering terror they carried his bones
in solemn procession to the sea
and cast him into the salt.

They unearthed a Lazarus
without a Christ to flesh him,
gave Christ a tomb unangeled
but as empty as his own.

It is nine hundred years
since the warrior was lost in the waves

and still one rises from his grave,
from the fluorescent's pale refrigerator light,
eyes cringing in the sun and poppies,
carrying a darkness on hands and clothes,

while somewhere the warrior wanders
in anger alone, cast out by Christ,
his bones tumbling like dice in the waves
this earth his empty reliquary
where for nine hundred years
they have grown their wheat out of his grave.

A T Joint

We lived underground.
The pipes ran overhead turning
elbows in the middle of the ceiling
toward some utility.

He had one and a half arms.
Part of a tattoo had been shot off.
It drained blue into a kissed pucker
where there was no angle.

I held beer cans for his leverage
but never asked and was told nothing
except his voice winding like insulation
round and round the pipes.

Tonight I am able to
remember my stunted pillow but
not his name or why it was we
joined away.

Impressions

for my son

I pluck the leaves and print them.
See. These are the ligaments of life,
sealed from the stamp-pad to page,
ink ruts the fluted module of the ginkgo,
transplanted from chlorophyll to pulp.

I guide you through the park
entering these designs into your book.
But this is only an outline
leaf to leaf. Turn the page.

We discard them
their veins dying in the stain of our proof.
And then comes the reversal.
The spore of life tracks us.
It clasps the wind behind our heels,
scraping the concrete with a sound that smothers
our hands in a cocoon of grave wrappings.

As we walk away to that spindling echo
I remember the cave in Spain;
the bison propped against the wall
tacky as half coagulated blood
after how many thousand years?
An animal of life's desire leaned against stone.
The fingerprints still wet upon its flank.

The Architect

Whatever his dreams have been it is now hard to say,
perhaps to build the last cathedral for an age
watching God depart — the light gone left windows glass —
so that he might say, I have given you domes and altars,
I can praise no more and will not go within to beg.

But the lust that carved fingers round a pencil
has worn down, a chiseled saint caressed into his stone,
the wash of a water-color sky that pales
into the pure primary fact of blankest paper.

It was so much more difficult than he thought,
not just bricks and mortar, but wives and children.
There was no commanding the kaleidoscope to stop.
The pieces kept on falling in and out.

Now he walks his property under lean boughed trees,
where clouds are torn in the naked snare of twigs,
and marks for the ax those that could not survive,
feeling the grass crisp with frost beneath his feet.

The leaves curl black over the hidden embers
but he sees above the haze of memory sharp and warm,
the wild ducks in arcs of numbers fly so low
that he hears the wind that cries through feathered wings.

The Phosphorescent Man

The smell of roast beef and browning potatoes
grew stronger, caught in the dimness of the stairwell
between the street door's stained glass and
the climb to the dining room, where my father
was a black and white unrecognizable child
with a collie above the sideboard,
and the old woman who lived alone with a brass bedstead,
huddled in her furniture —
all that was left after time and death.

Her face was a blurred baked apple
surrounded by the canaries' fluff —
dandelions of song wired in the window's sun.
Under the table her black shoes hid
with her arthritic legs
that bloated above the laces
into pastry bags of pain.

But I never knew him because he died
before I was two, before my memory
could arrange him to the trophy of a grandpa,
as she became grandma with a foreign voice,
canaries, a silver creamer and crippled legs.

Grandma and Grandpa,
one sound and one silence,
as light is to shadow, presence to absence,

conscious to unconscious,
fact to the dark nimbus that is not knowledge,
but is fishhooked with questions,
always they divide.
She is visible.
He is the phosphorescent man.

In the Brooklyn house where I first found
I wanted to find him, her silver
was behind my glass face on the corner cupboard.
His books hung in their black bindings
cracking in the steam heat —
Kierkegaard, Schopenhauer, Swedenborg —
behind my breath on the bookcases' glass doors.

To see, to touch, that is all I know of him.
The rest is photographs, a wedding moustache
and a man holding my father for a Sunday photograph
in a dustless curling brim beyond the frame.
Beyond that there are other people's stories.

My father remembers his father,
a man who preferred Brooklyn to his patrimony
of acres by the Baltic Sea,
eating the roast beef in silence,
walking down to the basement
past the banistered angles
while his wife played the piano.

He read before the furnace's open door —
alone with the flames and the page.

The piano far away, compartment by compartment
of floors and ceilings, sang to the wired yellow wings
as the coal settled into ash and clinkers
until she rang him to bed with a silver knife on the radiator.

She snuffed out the canaries
with hoods made from leftover bits of curtain
and covered the keys of her music.
He banked the fire, closed the furnace door.

The clang of embers followed his finger
in its place in the book,
up the banisters' barred shadows as he
put out the lights landing by landing.

I see him as my father tells it,
but I know him the way the artist knows Plato's Ideal —
a second removed remembrance —
a picture of a man,
a story of a man.

Some people have graves but some have only stones
and you cannot bring them the ransom
of flowers or flags on appropriate days
because you do not know where they died.

Someone walked alone in his own where,
after the music was over
and the coals caught their burnt out stones in the grate,
he extinguished the shadows lamp by lamp that
clung to the stair obstinate as salt.

PART THREE

Come with Me into Winter's Disheveled Grass

Come with me into winter's disheveled grass.
Bittersweet beads against the unhinged and barren apple
    tree.
Inside its gored trunk a last wad of snow lingers.

I give you a burr spined like a sea urchin.
You give me the split womb of the milkweed.

Together we will gather the hunter's cartridges
strewn across the frozen earth.
Red for you.
Green for me.
How the cylinders glow their hollows in the sun
now that death is gone.

Bridges

The bridges, legged like staples,
hitch the land together and the river
blunders between.

Our shadows fall over the wall
through the skewing wings of small gulls;
fall into the current, curdling
sudden splutters of froth.

But we are not taken out to sea, only
lie darkly, a stain immobile on the tide.

When we walk away, a syncopation of strides,
dragging our blotches behind us —
iron filings following beyond bridges —

elbow to elbow what do
our mitered arms mean? What is
this fastening, soil to soil,
as we ebb over the sidewalk?

The Quarrel

You sit behind your coffee.
I sit behind mine.
Our eyes are inside us.

Silence lies stale between us
on this morning whose heat is rent
by the singular shrill of a cicada.

And stale as a warped slice of bread is our quarrel,
and oppressive as this August morning is our love,
that mute as a moth with a torn wing,
lurches a path across the table.

Murder, a Love Poem

"You see it had to be done,"
I say, watching the blood wisp
downstream from my darning needle —
a convolvulus red tracer that wanes
into the current.

"There isn't another way,"
I whisper gently to your head
still as a dead rabbit on my lap.
My darning needle becomes a darning needle
and flies away.

"Growing things need humus,"
I explain as I shake spurred
grass seed to a silence of your eyes —
one punctured red — while my eyes are
innocent as soil.

Why Didn't Anyone Tell Hester Prynne?

Pity him up to his waist in middle age,
neither celibate nor pervert in ceramics, only ultimate
with a finger caught in the clay cookie jar.

Leading her under the slatted moonlight
of palm trees, opening, shutting,
like a nervous venetian blind —
he said shyly,
"Have you ever done this before?"
She said, "No,"
curling her toes expectantly into the sand.
God sighed relief through his grey beard.

I don't know what happened to him. But she went home,
a smug pendulum of skirts, to inform her husband,
who had angelic nightmares ever after,
"Gabriel told me to."

Deception Pass

for Judy and Mark Kawasaki

It is very high here
where the Pacific limbs blue between the islands
among rocks scabbed with grey lichens.

A grey crotchet of lichens,
the humble one-celled union of land and sea —
alga and fungus — works stone.

There is a photograph of the world, taken from outer
      space,
that resembles this rock,
a thing tender in its clasp of cloud and continent.

Their gentle chisel of growth
casts the rock to earth circle by circle,
an expanding scab of life,

and all their progeny are sand,
as if the earth were an ever-after hourglass
with this frail lace the only supplier of time.

This pale marriage clasps the eternal and makes it tick,
makes forever green
hours of trees

forever half-grown in the Pacific wind
where the serene shadow of a gull
lingers upon this thigh of tide.

A Poem for Lovers and Other Poets

Words ride my voice like children's sailboats
nodding into the civilized ripples of a park lake.
They pretend they are what I want to say to you.
Miniatures of emotion on a string of meaning,
a kite instead of wings.
My voice yanks at them
trying to free them to her own wind.

But words are only the toys of sense,
children's blocks for cathedrals of thought,
to be built, knocked down, and built again.
Even my spraddled hairpins on the rug
say more in their wrenched steel silence than my mouth.

And then you say my name,
a sound smothered between my neck and hair;
not an echo made by my mother,
say it again as though you are
chanting Eurydice into the sun,
chanting me into a June day of salt, of blue tart air.
And I become my voice,
a gull's moon slivered wing beneath you.

Poem

When night comes down,
and Manhattan is a net of fixed fireflies
separate in the dark,
not to have your arms is
to remember,
in the call of the flute
that catches its echo across my courtyard
in a duet of loneliness,
between sheets sweet with our double odor,
love.

Love in Black and White

My mouth salty with the taste of your flesh,
we lie tangled — sand and sea wrack.
Your arms the color
of my mother's cocoa,
of April earth
fresh under the harrow,
of all the bark of all the trees
I have loved
stark under a winter sun.
In this half light of love
my flesh is a pale shadow of yours,
as though night cast a moon ghost —
paper origami patterns of thighs and knees —
my skin a moth wing of your dusk.

But the stain of us
on the inside of my thigh
is colorless —
an egg white albumen etch
or the glue children use to cement model airplanes,
make-believes of wings and bombs.
Quiet as light we lie upon my thigh,
a Sesame of all the seeds
we will not give the sun
drying to a puckering scab.
And as the dawn dissolves our half light
back to the definitions of black and white
our mouths meet once more
across the sparrow's waking.

The Eclipse

It was getting dark
as we walked across the park.
Children and adults
with pieces of cardboard
waited on the grass for the eclipse:

waited to center the sun,
pull it through a pinhole
threading it over their shoulder
onto a blank piece of paper —
a reaction of an action like a poem.

But we did not wait.
Too eager for each other
to care about heaven's chiaroscuro
we scattered our shoes
like Saturday afternoon beer cans

and while those outside
focused the concentric shadings —
circle of corona and circle of penumbra —
on the secondary cause of paper
so as not to go primarily blind

we, with the somber sky,
shadow on shadow, without
the security of secondary interventions,
while sun and moon coaxialed obscurity,
fell flesh to flesh into sightlessness.